LION CUBS

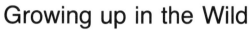

Growing up in the Wild

☐ **Books for Young Explorers**

NATIONAL GEOGRAPHIC SOCIETY

After a rain lions gather beside a puddle
in East Africa for a cool drink.
A long time ago, the roar of these great cats

could be heard in many parts of the world.
Now it breaks the stillness only in Africa,
and in a very small part of India.

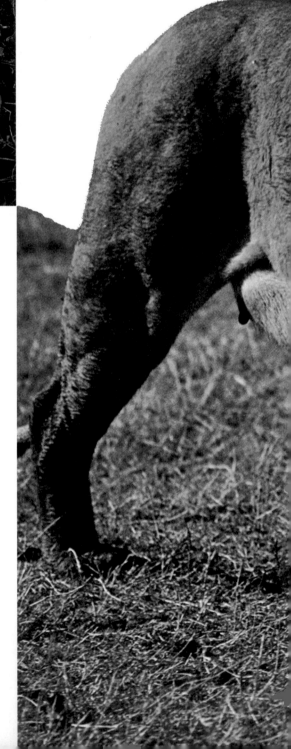

When cubs are born, their mother hides them in thick brush or in a rocky place to keep them safe. The newborn lions each weigh three or four pounds. Their eyes are usually closed, and their woolly brown fur is marked with many spots. The cubs' eyes open within a week, and the spots fade away as the cubs grow up.

ometimes the mother lion moves her cubs from one hiding place to another. Gripping them by the neck, she carries them firmly but gently in her teeth.

The lioness does not stay with her cubs all the time. Sometimes she leaves them while she goes off to hunt or to be with other lions of her group.

When their mother is away, the young cubs keep quiet and still. If they were noisy, leopards or hyenas might find them and kill them for food.

Like all young animals, lion cubs seem to be hungry most of the time. For the first few weeks of their lives their only food is their mother's milk. She usually lies patiently while they nurse. She may even feed cubs that are not her own.

But once in a while she may feel grumpy and out of sorts. Then she snarls impatiently when a hungry cub comes along looking for a meal. As impatient as its mother, the cub may snarl right back.

After a month or six weeks the cubs are old
enough to come out and meet other members
of the lion group, which is called a pride.
Lions are the only members of the cat family
that live together in a group.
 The big, shaggy-maned males do not play
with the cubs very much. But they help to protect
them, and often share meat with them.

When they are not eating or sleeping, lion cubs spend a lot of time playing. One curious little lion finds a tortoise and rolls it back and forth. Two others practice stalking, pouncing, and wrestling. They are learning skills they will need to become good hunters.

Cubs sun themselves while a patient lioness stands guard. Perhaps she sees a herd of antelopes in the distance.

Lions share their African home with many other animals. They hunt some of them for food. These young animals will never be playmates with lion cubs!

Like its mother, the young giraffe runs swiftly from danger. The little baboon rides on its mother's back for safety, while the 300-pound baby elephant is protected by its huge relatives.

As the cubs grow larger and stronger, they travel with the pride and learn how to hunt. Young lions start to eat meat when they are about six weeks old,

but they will not become successful hunters until they
are nearly two years old. Until then, older lions
share their kills with young ones in the pride.

Hunting can be hard work. After spotting its prey, a lion creeps slowly toward it, then charges and strikes it down. The zebra broke loose and ran away. Then the hungry lioness had to start again to find food for herself and for her family.

There are few water holes
in dry country, and lions and
other animals sometimes go two or
three days without a drink. But
no matter how thirsty they are,
most African animals usually wait
for a lion to finish drinking
before they approach a water hole.
They are safe as long as they keep
their distance, for they
can run faster than the lion.
 After the lion leaves,
other animals finally come to drink—
the boldly striped zebra,
the long-legged giraffes, and
the fleet-footed antelopes.

A mighty yawn means the beginning of another nap. This lion is sleepy because he has eaten a huge meal. Lions spend many hours every day sleeping or resting. They lie down in any shade they can find to escape the heat of the midday sun.

The lion's family in the animal kingdom includes
many different cats — even the house tabby.
The brightly spotted jaguar rests on a limb.
The cheetah runs at speeds up to 60 miles an hour.
The American mountain lion, or puma, can leap 20 feet
at a single bound. The lynx prowls the snowy woods
on big, fur-padded paws that act as snowshoes.
The tiger is often considered the most powerful cat.

JAGUAR

CHEETAH

MOUNTAIN LION

LYNX

TIGER

Sometimes a lion cub becomes lost, or is deserted
by its mother. Raising such a cub is no easy job
for the person who finds it. It must be bottle-fed
every few hours, and like other kittens, it often uses
its needle-sharp claws. It looks playful as it romps
in the grass, but it will soon grow large and dangerous.

Grown lions may be ferocious, but they are often gentle and tender with each other. These lions are mates. After a few months

the lioness will have a family of two to
six cubs. And when they grow up, the cubs
will take their turn as the king of beasts.

Prepared by the Special Publications Division of the National Geographic Society
Melvin M. Payne, President; Melville Bell Grosvenor, Editor-in-Chief; Gilbert M. Grosvenor, Editor.

Illustrations Credits

Richard D. Estes (page 1); George B. Schaller (2-3, 9, 10, 18-19, 20, 24-25); Burt Glinn, Magnum (4); Norman Myers, Bruce Coleman Inc. (5, 6, 13, 21, 24); Volkmar Wentzel, National Geographic Staff (7); Leonard Lee Rue III, Bruce Coleman Inc. (8); Joan and Alan Root (12 top); Mark N. Boulton, Bruce Coleman Inc. (12 bottom); Alan Root (14-15, 28, 29); Hugo van Lawick (16, 17 bottom); Judy Houry (17 top); George Holton, Photo Researchers, Inc. (22-23); Walter Chandoha (26); National Geographic Artist Ned M. Seidler (26-27); Sally Foster (30-31).

Cover photograph: Karl H. Maslowski
Endsheets: Arlinka Blair